NEW YORK REVIEW COMICS

ALMOST COMPLETELY BAXTER

GLEN BAXTER is the author of many books since the 1970s, including *The Impending Gleam*, *The Billiard Table Murders*, and *Blizzards of Tweed*. His work has appeared in *The New Yorker*, *Vanity Fair*, *Elle*, *Vogue*, *Le Monde*, *The Observer*, and *The Independent on Sunday*. He is a Chevalier of the Order of Arts and Letters, and his art is often exhibited in New York, Amsterdam, Paris, and London, where "Colonel" Baxter lives.

MARLIN CANASTEEN is the author of *The Balearic Trilogy* and the acclaimed biography of the great American poet Richard Griffin. His books have been translated into fifteen languages. For many years he acted as Security Advisor at the Bolick Mandolin Conservation Society in Duluth, Minnesota. He currently resides in Toledo, Ohio.

THIS IS A NEW YORK REVIEW COMIC
PUBLISHED BY THE NEW YORK REVIEW OF BOOKS
435 Hudson Street, New York, NY 10014
www.nyrb.com

Library of Congress Cataloging-in-Publication Data

Names: Baxter, Glen, artist.
Title: Almost completely Baxter : new and selected blurtings / by Glen Baxter
 ; illustrated by Glen Baxter.
Description: New York : New York Review Comics, 2016. | Description based on
 print version record and CIP data provided by publisher; resource not
 viewed.
Identifiers: LCCN 2015039117 (print) | LCCN 2015036292 (ebook) | ISBN
 9781590179864 (epub) | ISBN 9781590179857 (hardback)
Subjects: LCSH: English wit and humor, Pictorial. | BISAC: HUMOR / Form /
 Comic Strips & Cartoons. | COMICS & GRAPHIC NOVELS / General.
Classification: LCC NC1479.B29 (print) | LCC NC1479.B29 A4 2016 (ebook) | DDC
 741.65/2--dc23
LC record available at http://lccn.loc.gov/2015039117

ISBN 978-1-59017-985-7
Available as an electronic book; ISBN 978-1-59017-986-4

Printed in China
10 9 8 7 6 5 4 3 2 1

ALMOST
COMPLETELY BAXTER

NEW AND SELECTED BLURTINGS

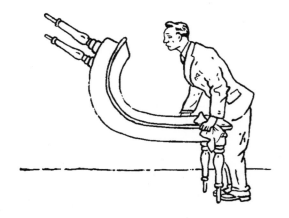

GLEN BAXTER

Introduction by
MARLIN CANASTEEN

NEW YORK REVIEW COMICS · *New York*

"HOW ABOUT I TOSS ON ANOTHER BAXTER?" DRAWLED THE CONNOISSEUR

INTRODUCTION

AS A YOUNG cub reporter I was given my first assignment—to interview the man they call Colonel Baxter. I packed my notepad and pencil and headed out for the grounds of the Baxter residence in a remote corner of South London. The taxi screeched to a halt at the perimeter fence. The driver refused my money and roared off into the murk.

I stepped forward to peruse the ring of antique Chinese cannons guarding the dilapidated topiary hedges that led to the first of a series of sentry boxes. After passing through several checkpoints, I found myself on the terrace of a crumbling Victorian mansion. I rang the doorbell and a butler ushered me into the entrance hall where an ornate crest announced TOFU WALK WITH ME.

Within a matter of minutes, the great man appeared, removed his pith helmet, and extended his hand towards me. "Come in," he announced, "and take a seat here."

I crossed the floor and following Baxter's instructions took a seat in a wickerwork bath chair, which he assured me was an exact replica of the one in which Annie B. Hore traveled to Africa whilst writing her magnum opus, *To Lake Tanganyika in a Bath Chair*.

He motioned towards a large, slightly faded map of the world.

"This is Yorkshire!" Baxter bellowed, pointing to a charred oblong just above Oslo. I realized I was in the presence of greatness, or, at the very least, a maniac.

"Tea?" he continued, indicating the door to the library. Oak-panelled bookshelves were lined with leather-bound volumes bearing such titles as *Snake for Supper* by Fred Baxter and *Elk Hunting in Sweden* by George Washington Baxter.

I nervously pulled out my trusted Platinum Press Man pencil and my notepad of soiled napkins, and exhaled my first question: "Colonel Baxter, where did it begin?"

"Like many things," he roared, "in Leeds. I started drawing and clay modelling at my nursery school, the Royal Hunslet Academy for Dishevelled Tykes. At the end of term there was an Open Day and my parents came along to see how the work of the children there.

"There were three trestle tables on display, covered with lots of tiny clay figures. My parents asked the teacher, 'Which ones were made by our son, Glen?' The teacher replied: 'These two tables.'

"Clearly the alarm bells were already sounding. . ."

I jockeyed for my next answer: "Were there unexpected hurdles on the race course of your life?"

Baxter replied: "I had a stammer. One day my mother sent me on an errand to buy a collar stud for my father's shirt. I was very nervous and began to practice my speech as I walked slowly down the hill to the shop. I marched in, full of confidence and said, quite fluently, 'Can I buy a collar stud, please?' The shopkeeper looked down at the young boy standing before him and answered, 'I'm very sorry. Perhaps the shop next door can help you.' I turned and made my exit, discovering as I did that I had been standing in a furniture shop.

"As I overcame my stammer, I became obsessed with the words that had once tripped me up—the way they looked on paper and the way they sounded enthralled me." The Colonel stared at me, enunciating words that shook my ears:

"Wimple."

"Blurt."

"Desperado."

"Bagel."

I slouched in awe, but pressed forward with my queries: "What else drove you down your life's reckless path? Where did you learn your notorious craft? The back alleys of Leeds? The docks of Bridlington? The caverns of Sheffield?"

The Colonel's eyes twinkled as he growled, "Films were shown continuously—newsreels, shorts, and, of course, B movies, which were almost always black-and-white cowboy films. The exploits of Tom Mix, Gabby Hayes, and Ming the Merciless took place in a world of fractured narrative: we used to enter cinemas whilst the films were already show-ing, sit down in the middle of a film, watch it right through then on again till the part where you came in popped up!"

Looking to fill out my piece, I launched a softball inquiry: "Once you were grown, what came next?"

"I applied to art school in Leeds, desperate to shake off the monotony of school life. Once there, however, I discovered that most of the teach-ing centered around producing vapid versions of American Abstract Im-pressionism. I felt completely out in the cold and leapt eagerly into the clandestine, warm embrace of Dada and Surrealism. Years passed by in a flurry of chiaroscuro and vermillion before I left and made my way down to London on a makeshift sled. I discovered the work of Frank O'Hara and it wasn't long before I was tumbling into the murky twilight world of po-etry. I began to dabble in prose poems, picking up mimeographed poetry magazines in Charing Cross Road.

"I submitted some early attempts to *Adventures in Poetry*, a little magazine edited by Larry Fagin at the Poetry Project at St. Mark's Church in New York City. I soon received an invitation to visit America."

I interrupted, blurting out: "Was this what led you to become the first Baxter to cross the Atlantic?"

Colonel Baxter merely pointed to a black-and-white photo on his mantel: him, young and bare-chested, astride a flimsy-looking raft in the middle of the ocean.

"In 1974 I was invited over to read from my collected works at St. Mark's Church before an audience of poets, painters, and filmmakers. I stood at the lectern, dressed in a tweed suit, and began to speak. People burst into spontaneous laughter. I had arrived.

"I showed around some of my little ink drawings and that same year had my first exhibition in the world at the Gotham Book Mart Gallery."

My trusted pencil shot out of my hand in excitement: "Was this the point of the Baxter convergence of word and picture?"

Baxter waved his hand towards two ornately framed booklets: "Gotham Book Mart published two little stapled-together magazines:

Fruits of the World in Danger and *The Handy Guide to Amazing People.*

"Edward Gorey was a regular visitor and exhibitor at the Gotham Book Mart and he dropped by one of my shows there and bought a whole stack of drawings. He was very enthusiastic and it spurred me on: having your work bought by an artist you admire is as high as you can go on the Artistic Richter Scale.

"I was still having problems getting my work recognized in England and it took a brave Dutchman, Jaco Groot, to bring out my first book in Europe. *Atlas* was published in Amsterdam in 1979. Groot proudly sent out copies all across Holland. He sold six. He sat alone in his room, surrounded by trampled tulips, planning his revenge.

"Back home in London I was finally given the opportunity to unfurl my oeuvre at the Institute of Contemporary Arts and following that things really got out of hand. English and American publishers rushed to my door, the Tate Gallery bought a set of prints. My drawings appeared in *The Observer*, *The New Yorker* and the *Ilkley Tortoise Quarterly*. My art found its way into the homes of numerous dignitaries, submarine captains, notorious criminals, and John Cleese."

He laughed at the thought of this, his voice echoing down innumerable hallways. I urged him to continue, clutching my pencil tightly to my chest. A tennis ball bounced in through an open window and rolled away into the darkness at the end of the library.

Baxter stepped forward and began. "Then gradually things began to unravel," he explained. "My interest in marquetry was developing into an all-consuming passion, and it wasn't too long before I found myself wandering alone in a wilderness of twine and metal hasps."

He went on, setting the record straight on his mothball addiction and speaking in hushed tones of his incarceration in the mysterious ZIMMER 35 at the Furkablick Hotel high above Andermatt.

"It was quite a few years later that the French government discovered me and brought me back here."

The next four hours in his company seemed to fly by, as I was regaled with tales of his time with the Royal Ballet and his mentor Sir Frederick Ashton, and the strange events of the Alpine Ascent with a team of Bulgarian yodellers intent on learning the secret of Baxter's Triple Reverse Salchow.

As I finished scribbling and looked up, I found myself alone in the vast room. Colonel Baxter had disappeared, leaving only the scent of cordite and Earl Grey tea lingering in the air.

I grasped the sides of the bath chair before I lost consciousness. Two days later I found myself in a military hospital bed. A nurse was drawing a blanket over my arms. She handed me my notepad. It was blank apart from the letters U F O T scrawled across the cover. As she turned on her heel she looked at me and announced, "By the way, someone came in late last night and dropped this off for you."

There on my bedside table was a slightly foxed edition of *Shadow of a Gunhawk* by Shane V. Baxter. The nurse crossed to the door and closing it behind her whispered, "I think this is only the beginning." I switched off the light and drifted back into an uneasy sleep.

—MARLIN CANASTEEN
TOLEDO, OHIO

IT WAS PRECISELY SIX-FIFTEEN

"THESE PANTS ARE WELDED STEEL,"
ANNOUNCED THE STRANGER

THE TWINS INTRODUCED
THE IMPOSTOR

IT WAS HARVEY'S BOLD PLAN TO ARRIVE
AT THE ENEMY HEADQUARTERS AT
PORT ARTHUR UNDETECTED...

"I WHITTLE THESE!" BLURTED CRAIG

IT SEEMED TO AMUSE HIM, SO I
COMPLIED WITH HIS ODD REQUEST

THE DEAN WASN'T THERE ANYMORE

"WE'LL HAVE NO ALLITERATION IN THIS HERE BUNKHOUSE!" SNORTED McCULLOCH

"I KEEP MY BAGELS IN HERE"
WHISPERED THE DESPERADO

IT WAS THE SMALLEST PIZZA THEY HAD
EVER SEEN

"NOT SO FAST, VARLET — I DEMAND A SECOND
FITTING!" BELLOWED SIR PEREGRINE

GREAT FAILURES
OF OUR TIME

Nº 16

The First Yo-Yo

GREAT FAILURES
OF OUR TIME

*No. 77 First Dental Extraction
by Red Admiral*

IT WAS RUDOLPH'S TURN TO
LUBRICATE THE CINDERS

EVERY OTHER WEDNESDAY THE LADS
WERE ALLOWED AN EXTRA RATION

HE TOOK HER IN HIS ARMS AND
GENTLY SQUEEZED HER GOATEE

"SO YOU'RE THE MYOPIC MULDONI BOYS
FROM CHICAGO, EH?" SPAT LANNIGAN

FRUITS OF THE WORLD
IN
DANGER

Number 1   The Orange

IT WAS TOM'S FIRST BRUSH
WITH MODERNISM

VANCE LIVED IN CONSTANT FEAR
OF LOSING HIS WRISTWATCH....

IT WAS MRS. CRABTREE AND SHE WAS
IN NO MOOD FOR PLEASANTRIES

HE WAS FROM BROOKLYN ALL RIGHT

MIRANDA HAD STUMBLED UPON OUR
SUPPLY OF BEARDS.......

YOUNG TALBOT STOOD UP AND WITH A
SHRIEK OF TRIUMPH WHISKED OFF HIS
BOATER TO REVEAL THE FORBIDDEN
POMPADOUR......

HE HAD BEEN CAUGHT USING THE
FORBIDDEN "HEAD PEN" AGAIN.......

"1 SUPPOSE YOU'RE ALL WONDERING WHY
I'VE GATHERED YOU HERE TODAY"
WHISPERED THE BOSUN

THERE WAS STILL MUCH TO
LEARN ABOUT SZECHUAN
CUISINE

"I'LL THANK YOU TO STOP JUGGLING MY
GHERKINS!" SNORTED THE ANGUISHED THROGUE

JEDSON WAS NOTED FOR HIS WITHERING
SIDELONG GLANCES

YOUNG HANK ENTERTAINED THE BOYS
WITH A FINE DISPLAY OF SMOULDERING

GREAT FAILURES
OF OUR TIME

No. 224 The First Frankfurter

"I'M AFRAID IT'S GRIM NEWS,
SANDY— THE VICE-CONSUL
INTENDS TO BAN THE
WEARING OF WIMPLES
AFTER 7:15 P.M"

"WHAT HAVE YOU DONE WITH MY
WIMPLE?" GROWLED BIG 'BULL' HARPER

McGUIRE SEEMED TO HAVE RIDDEN
INTO A TRAP......

THE LOMAX BOYS KEPT UP AN ALL-NIGHT
VIGIL ON THE NOUGAT

SIR ROLAND TRIED TO CONVINCE THE
SCEPTICS OF THE POTENTIAL OF HIS
LIGHTWEIGHT "MINI-SHIELD".......

FRUITS OF THE WORLD
IN
DANGER

Number 2   *The Grape*

PECOS BILL HAD A "THING"
ABOUT HOUSEHOLD DUST.....

"I STUB MY CIGARS OUT........ THERE!"
SNORTED THE TEXAN

VERONICA HAD HIT UPON A SCHEME FOR
DEALING WITH BOLSOVER'S PACKED DEFENCE

"1 APPEAR TO HAVE LEFT YOUR SANDWICHES
BACK ON ALPHA IV, OLD MAN" HISSED BLAKE

THE SUMMER TERM WAS ALWAYS
A BITTER DISAPPOINTMENT

IAN WAS BECOMING IMPOSSIBLY JEALOUS. I FOUND
MYSELF HAVING TO MAINTAIN A ROUND-THE-
CLOCK VIGIL ON THE PIGTAIL

AS THE EVENING DEEPENED INTO TWILIGHT
AND HE FELT HIMSELF BECOME RESTLESS AND
FEVERISH, SCRUNDLEY TURNED ONCE AGAIN
TO THE HORN...

"IT APPEARS TO BE SOME KIND OF FANCY WALLPAPER" DRAWLED OLD THREPE

Strange Customs
of Many Lands

Vowel Study, St Agnes Eve
Brocklehampton

THERE WAS BARELY ENOUGH TIME FOR ME TO
CAST A CRITICAL EYE OVER THE SEAMWORK
ON HIS LEGGINGS...

YOUNG ROBERTS COULD NOT FACE ANOTHER MOUSSAKA

THE REDECORATION OF BASE CAMP
III WAS THE MOST PERILOUS ASPECT
OF THE ENTIRE EXPEDITION.

MANY WERE THE OCCASIONS WHEN I CHOSE
NOT TO PARTICIPATE IN THOSE EARNEST
AFTER-DINNER DEBATES

"DURING MY YEARS OUT EAST I MANAGED
TO PICK UP ONE OR TWO TIPS ON THE
ART OF RELAXATION" EXPLAINED HOLDSWORTH

IT WAS AT CHAUNDLEY CAMP THAT I
FIRST LEARNED TO SET FIRE TO MY OWN
KNEECAPS

FRUITS OF THE WORLD
IN
DANGER

Number 8   The Fig

PAYING ATTENTION

IT HAD TAKEN me a week to prepare for this. No one had the slightest suspicion that their tongues would be the subject of a police investigation, but there would be time enough for research and debate later. The dinghy rounded the headland with a great deal of movement. The Mate puffed greedily at his habit. It was not, after all, for him to criticize the catering at Port Moresby. At the centre of the recent upheavals and reciprocations stood a woman the like of which the islanders had not seen before. One arm longer than the other, reddish hair swept up in the breeze, she certainly commanded respect, fear, admiration, and disgust. The Mate ceased his tugging and looked at the Captain. He could not stop transforming his thoughts into a string of continuous disappointments. He pushed his forehead up and back. A plank, about seven feet long, remained inches away. He saw it twice. He had tried to reach it only once before, but that had been three weeks ago to the day, and for the moment he seemed content to remain where he stood, swaying over the liverwurst. If only he were able to reach out and take up the spatula, he might again be able to regain his composure. He knew this, but felt otherwise. His knees were rotating very slowly, and the smoke from the shore was already curling on his lower lip. He had led such a disgruntled existence that he had begun to enjoy the spectacle of a tumbler of water being filled, emptied, and filled again. A slow smile of gratification flashed into the air. It seemed to emanate from his chin, but he knew this was unlikely. He was evidently upset. He tumbled forward into a beaker of milk. This was his last chance. He grabbed his legs, and tucking them up under his collar, he rolled quietly into the harbour.

ALTHOUGH PETS WERE OFFICIALLY FORBIDDEN
THERE WERE THOSE WHO, WHEN DARKNESS
FELL, CHOSE TO IGNORE SCHOOL RULES

OUR MEETINGS WERE BECOMING MORE
AND MORE EMOTIONALLY CHARGED

MRS PRENDERGHAST HAD HER OWN WAY OF
TURNING EVERY MEAL INTO A SPECIAL OCCASION

SOMETIMES, AS A TREAT, WE WERE
ALLOWED TO LOOK AT A GLASS OF
WARM WATER FOR A FEW MINUTES

BALLANTINE CALCULATED THAT HE WAS
APPROACHING THE SAUERKRAUT AT AN
APPROXIMATE VELOCITY OF 78.6 M.P.H

WITH DEADLY ACCURACY YOUNG SILBURN
PICKED OUT THE WOODPECKER

BOYS WHO HAD FORGOTTEN THEIR
PROTRACTORS WERE SUBJECTED TO
MR LLOYD'S WALNUT ORDEAL

AFTER A FEW MONTHS I REALIZED IT WAS SIMPLY A DEVICE FOR SHOWING ME HIS THIGHS

SHARING MY SANDWICH WITH ERIC
MARKED THE BEGINNING OF A LONG,
SERIOUSLY TROUBLED WEEKEND

THE CONCEPT OF THE DIMMER SWITCH HAD
YET TO REACH THE LAZY K BUNKHOUSE

UNFORTUNATELY PIERRE HAD A
LONG HISTORY OF *STILTON ABUSE*

WITH ONE SWIFT AND DECISIVE MOVE
TOM REVEALED THE ILLICIT KUMQUATS

OCCASIONALLY THE TERRIFYING WHIRR OF
THE PORRIDGE-MAKING FACILITIES COULD
BE HEARD DOWN THE CORRIDOR

IT WAS MY FIRST VISIT
TO A DUTCH RESTAURANT

"SO YOU FOUND THE BUTTER, THEN?" GRUNTED KLAUS

TOGETHER WE WERE ABLE TO REMOVE
ALL TRACES OF THE INCRIMINATING TOFU

FRUITS OF THE WORLD
IN
DANGER

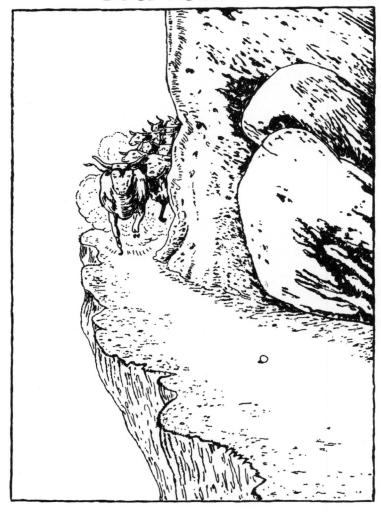

Number 10   The Apricot

AS ASHTRAYS GO, IT WAS
CERTAINLY QUITE IMPRESSIVE

THERE WAS NOTHING ERIC LIKED
BETTER THAN AN EVENING ALONE
AT HOME WITH HIS TWINE

ALONE IN HIS MOMENT OF
RAPTURE , RALPH RETURNED
ONCE AGAIN TO CONTEMPLATION
OF THE GOURD

GRADUALLY I BEGAN TO CONCUR
WITH HIS POINT OF VIEW

EDGAR HAD ATTENDED MANY
A POETRY EVENING

THERE WERE TIMES WHEN I BEGAN
TO TIRE OF POLISHING MR. THRONGUE

HUBERT GAZED ON IN AWE AT
THE MORSEL

AS COLLECTIONS OF TEETH GO, IT
WAS CERTAINLY IMPRESSIVE

I'LL NEVER FORGET THE DAY I
MET BRENDA

"THESE MARKS ARE ENTIRELY
CONSISTENT WITH A BILLIARD TABLE
BEING DRAGGED THROUGH HERE."

FROM HER ROOM, GLADYS SAW VERY LITTLE
OF THE SPLENDOURS OF VENICE.

HOW HE HATED SATURDAY
MORNING SHOPPING

AS A FIRST SEXUAL EXPERIENCE IT
HAD NOT BEEN A TOTAL DISAPPOINTMENT

ERIC WAS NOW BEGINNING TO WISH HE'D
RETURNED HIS OVERDUE LIBRARY BOOKS

OLD CATTERMOLE WAS OUT IN
THE GARDEN TENDING THE FUCHSIAS

SLOWLY, BUT WITH UNERRING PRECISION, DR. TUTTLE REACHED FOR HIS LUGER

"I'M AFRAID I'M GOING TO HAVE TO
SHOW YOU MY NIPPLE, YOUNG LAD"
ANNOUNCED THE CONSTABLE GRAVELY

I LIKED TO THINK THAT OURS WAS
A RATHER SPECIAL RELATIONSHIP

IT WAS THEN THAT MR. CLUMBERS
TOOK IT UPON HIMSELF TO
INSTRUCT US IN THE ART OF
SHOPLIFTING

FROM TIME TO TIME, UNCLE WILF FROM CLEETHORPES WOULD PAY US ONE OF HIS FAMOUS "UNEXPECTED VISITS"....

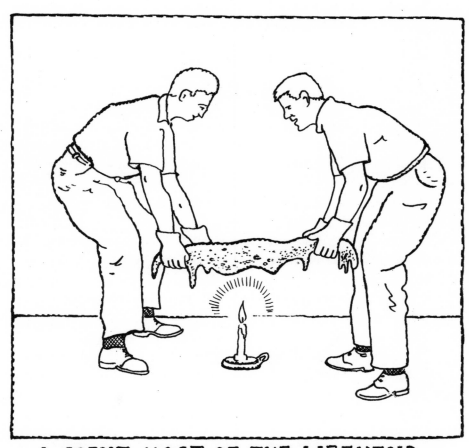

I SPENT MOST OF THE WEEKEND
ASSISTING BRIAN WITH HIS OMELETTES

SUNSET OVER DUDLEY

THE PORTUGUESE loomed up from behind an overturned stroganoff. His legs seemed unsteady. His name was Vrom. "All right, Angela," he was saying. Her fork dropped into the broccoli. She had only a split second to make her move.

"I've got a hunch you're in some kind of trouble . . ." she began.

He waved a tiny jewelled axe at her.

"And you've been talking to that Sinclair Duggan again, haven't you," she added, rolling her tongue round the double g in Duggan.

"Uh uh," he replied.

"Not romantic, but typical," she noted. There was thought mirrored now in her flashing eyes.

"You can get back to your meal now," she hissed.

He tore off in the direction of the kitchen. His eyes were dark and his mouth clamped to a thin grey line. It seemed as if in one flash his thought had crystallized into adamant resolve. This time he knew it, though.

"What is romance without finance?" he asked, pounding his clenched fists into his tweed blouson. It was some time before his cogitations ceased.

In the bustle of those first few hours at the surgery, Angela had sensed the beginnings of a thrill. Her colleagues had noticed it too, and there had been one or two ugly scenes before the lighting track was replaced. The flushed, sheepish faces had not deterred her, for alone she knew the agony of long, wet afternoons listening to other people's complaints.

The door swung open. The Portuguese was back.

"Nut?" he inquired.

It seemed an odd feast, but yet she complied.

"I was delayed until I came," he added, sitting down next to her.

94

The brooding senior jerked to life. Angela realized he had become a public danger, and now, with the Portuguese by her side also, she felt decidedly uneasy. The Portuguese leaned over.

"Fond of pets?" he queried. "I can arrange things."

For upwards of a minute a strange feeling of disinterest flooded the room. Then Angela spoke.

Kirk, despite his impediment, had managed to reach the sofa. He had left Tucson only that morning. Now he was urging another visit to the roof. The clanging of bells was what he longed for most. Angela knew this and shied a slipper in his direction.

Kirk caught it in his teeth.

"It's all I crave," he beamed, "and more than I could expect."

"Then here you go," Angela growled, and tossed over another.

Kirk expressed his approval with a somewhat more dulcet grunt than was usual. His nostrils dilated with pleasure and he began to slump.

The unwanted clamour and sign of delight had evidently unnerved the Portuguese. He was taking deep breaths and counting with his fingers. Angela recognized the symptoms.

"Dr. Judd will see you now," she said, pointing to the door.

"You scug," he exploded, "I'm off."

That was the last that Angela ever saw of him. She peeled off her coat and began to retrace her steps until she came up to the dangling rope. She stopped here to admire the view. A chill wind was whistling across a gigantic expanse of mud beyond which lay a man-made gully decorated with red and white bunting. It had been a long time since Angela had dusted there, and the slogan SEX FOR NEW BOYS was only a distant memory now.

WE MADE OUR WAY UP THROUGH
CONTEMPORARY FICTION AND ON
TO THE CAPUCCINO MACHINE

THE EASTER EGG HUNT AT LOWER CHEDLEY
WAS KNOWN TO BE ONE OF THE TOUGHEST
IN THE WHOLE OF WILTSHIRE

ARNOLD BROWNSTEIN, DRIVING SOUTH

ALONG THE HIGHWAY, SUDDENLY
REALIZES HE IS IN BIG TROUBLE

AND WITH THE SITUATION RAPIDLY

DETERIORATING, PULLS OFF THE ROAD.

ALL 1 HAD TO DO NOW WAS
TO COAX THEM INTO THE NET

"ARE YOU READY TO EMBRACE VEGETARIANISM?"
SNAPPED THE REGULATOR

18 BUTTERFLIES IN UNDER

SIX AND A HALF SECONDS.

"RUMOUR HAS IT YOU'VE BEEN TRANSFERRED
TO INTELLIGENCE, SNEDLEY"

BIG AL WASN'T ABOUT
TO TAKE ANY CHANCES

I DEFTLY SKETCHED IN THE
FINER POINTS OF MY THESIS

UNFORTUNATELY, LUNCH WAS SERVED
ALMOST IMMEDIATELY

"WHEN YOU HAVE A SPARE MOMENT, I'D LIKE TO RAISE THE SUBJECT OF INVASION OF PERSONAL SPACE" SPLUTTERED OLAF

THINGS JUST DIDN'T SEEM TO BE
GOING ROB'S WAY...

"I SUPPOSE YOU REALIZE THIS SHADOW IS ILLEGAL?" BARKED THE BOSUN

HE SEEMED TO THINK I HAD
NEVER SWEPT A FLOOR BEFORE

BY THE TUMBLERS

A BRILLIANT IDEA shot into Nick's head. He closed his eyes with his feet, turned, and opened the bathroom door. Barry put his head on his shoulder. Even if he were completely straight Nick could sense the incessant quaking.

At the appropriate moment, Barry closed the bathroom door. Water shot from all the tiny holes in his duffel bag. Nick's lips weren't moving. He wasn't thinking but he could see the beekeeper.

"I am bad," he said.

"I am German, so of course I know that," replied Nick.

The red vinyl seat squeaked a little as they turned on the floor. "I wanted to go to dinner," explained the beekeeper.

"Only two more hours," Nick told him, kicking off his shoes.

A small boy came towards them, turned to Barry, and climbed slowly up to his armpits. He wondered if he dared ask for a ride.

The outlook was not at all encouraging. With sudden resolve, Nick moved forward. It was ten o'clock. The beekeeper pressed a bell, nudging his little cap in salute, then looked at the border again. He saw the bowl of unripe raspberries and thought no more of it. "We have important things to do," announced Nick, on the verge of tears. He reached up to the bathroom shelf and took it. The rusty metal 4 had been nailed to the edge. He began to explore this new shape.

There was a danger of taking too much at once, he realized. He groaned as the others trod. With a little glow of happiness he saw the upper part of Barry's face move slightly. He would never forget.

"Thank you very much," he said.

Barry put his foot on his shoulder, confident he could get away with

111

it. To go by the Tumblers was his ultimate aim but he knew now that time was running out.

Whenever he looked anyone in the face a little bell chimed. The beekeeper nodded and grinned. He would not be seen to breathe without assistance and Barry was only too happy to oblige. Speaking only Italian was an option now.

"You don't have shoes," barked Nick.

Stray dogs with ugly snouts paraded by outside, unaware of the terror on Barry's face, wrapped now in a dark green towel. Like lights at a carnival, the music suddenly went out. Evening had fallen.

Carts piled high with turnips followed the dogs down the street. Ant-like men were tooting their wooden flutes.

With the aid of two sticks, Nick bolted from the room.

Words he was only just beginning to learn passed through his head as he ran. The beekeeper followed, wondering which one would tell the other about the pulley.

Barry put his head on his shoulder and before long his tongue was rotating rapidly, taut as a piano wire, but somehow less attractive. At least the beekeeper had the good grace to acknowledge this and stopped briefly, gleaming in the dark.

"LET ME EXPLAIN HOW THIS WORKS"
ANNOUNCED PROFESSOR DRUNDLE

"YOU'D BETTER HAVE A DAMNED GOOD EXCUSE
FOR BEING OUT OF UNIFORM THIS TIME,
WAINWRIGHT!" BARKED THE SERGEANT

CLANDESTINE MEETINGS OF THE
JANE AUSTEN SOCIETY WERE
HELD EVERY OTHER THURSDAY

CHRIS WAS DETERMINED TO SECURE ANOTHER
MERIT BADGE FOR HIS BŒUF BOURGUINON

HE WAS A FIRM BELIEVER
IN CONVENIENCE FOODS

DADDY SEEMED TO BE RUNNING
A LUCRATIVE LITTLE SIDELINE
CHURNING OUT MONDRIANS

THERE REMAINED A CYNICAL MINORITY
WHO BELIEVED OUR CONTEST WAS RIGGED

JANET SET ASIDE AN HOUR
EACH DAY TO WORK ON HER
THREATENING LETTERS

THE WHEELS OF PROGRESS SEEMED TO
BE SPINNING JUST A TAD TOO QUICKLY
FOR BIG JAKE McCULLOUGH

"BUT THIS IS THE PROPERTY YOU BOUGHT
ON THE INTERNET" EXPLAINED SERGEI

ROBIN NOTICES A DISTURBING NEW
TREND SWEEPING THROUGH SHERWOOD

"PERMISSION TO MOISTURIZE, SIR?"

YOUNG NEVILLE'S FIRST NOVEL CERTAINLY
BROUGHT A WELCOME GLOW INTO OUR
OTHERWISE DRAB AND DREARY LIVES

IT WAS CERTAINLY AN IMPRESSIVE
COLLECTION OF PORNOGRAPHY, MARRED
ONLY BY THE LACKLUSTRE SECTION
DEVOTED TO LATE SPRING VEGETABLES

I COULD SEE CLEARLY HE HAD NOTHING TO SAY

SEX EDUCATION LESSONS WERE LEFT IN THE
CAPABLE HANDS OF MRS GRISWOLD

"IT'S THE SECOND CHAPTER OF 'Á LA
RECHERCHE DU TEMPS PERDU'..."
EXPLAINED BIG JAKE

" 'TIS CALLED POLENTA, ROBIN, AND
AS A FLOOR COVERING IT HAS NO
EQUAL" EXPLAINED THE SALESMAN

I DELIBERATED FOR A MOMENT
THEN DECIDED TO GIVE HIM
THE FULL 300,000 VOLTS

IT IS DECEMBER AND ALREADY
DARK FORCES ARE GATHERING

I LIVED IN CONSTANT FEAR OF
AN OUTBREAK OF YODELLING

SHAKING OFF THE McGUIRE
BOYS WAS NEVER EASY

THERE WERE THOSE IN THE VILLAGE
WHO SUSPECTED HERR GRINDLE MIGHT
BE HARBOURING A DARK SECRET

I SENSED IMMEDIATELY THAT 1 WAS IN
THE PRESENCE OF A MAN UNUSED TO
THE CONSTRAINTS OF RATIONAL DISCOURSE

IT BECAME A RACE AGAINST TIME
TO FINISH THE DEATH RAY
BEFORE THE THREATENED ARRIVAL
OF GREAT UNCLE BERNARD

THERE WERE TIMES WHEN I
BEGAN TO THINK I MIGHT JUST
BE IN THE WRONG PROFESSION

I HAD THE DISTINCT FEELING
THAT CELIA WAS GOING OUT OF
HER WAY TO ANNOY ME...

THE SITUATION WAS DETERIORATING
RAPIDLY...

"MIGHT I BE CORRECT IN ASSUMING THAT A SINGLE, WAYWARD SPARK COULD WIPE OUT 18 MONTHS OF WORK ON YOUR MATCHSTICK MASTERPIECE, DAD?"

MOST OF MY CHILDHOOD WAS SPENT
AVOIDING GREEN VEGETABLES

IT WOULD TAKE A LITTLE TIME, BUT
TOGETHER WE MIGHT JUST BE ABLE
TO DIGEST THE COLLECTED WORKS
OF ALBERTO MANGUEL

BIBLIOGRAPHY

This bibliography has been culled from the archives of the British Museum Reading Room, London, and the Library, University of Texas at Austin.

ALICE MARY BAXTER
Adventure Comes to Brack-
endene

ALLAN MUIR BAXTER
The Distribution of Load
along Nuts
The Fatigue of Bolts and Studs

ANDREW BAXTER
Thoughts on Dreaming
An Enquiry into the Nature of
the Human Soul
Matho; sive cosmoth eoria
puerilis

ANNE BAXTER
Intermission: a true story

ANNETTE KAR BAXTER
Henry Miller, expatriate

ARCHIBALD BAXTER
We Will Not Cease

SIR ARTHUR BEVERLEY
BAXTER
The Blower of Bubbles
First Nights and Footlights
Strange Street

BATSELL BARRETT BAXTER
Speaking for The Master

BERNICE BAXTER
Group Experience: The
Democratic Way
Growth in Human Relations

BERTRAM BAXTER
Stone Blocks and Iron Rails

BRIAN NEWLAND BAXTER
Teach Yourself Naval Archi-
tecture

BRUCE LEE BAXTER
An Elliptic Function Solution
of the Nonlinear Differential

Equation of Motion in
Synchronous Machines

C.E. BAXTER
Talofa

CHARLES BAXTER
Chameleon

CHARLES HOMER BAXTER
Examination and Valuation of
Mineral Property by Baxter
and Parks

CHARLES NEWCOMB
BAXTER
Boston Athenaeum

CHERRIE FULLER BAXTER
A Study of Administration
of Old Age Assistance in
Douglas County

CRAIG BAXTER
District Voting Trends in
India. A Research Tool
The Jana Sangh
Servants of the Sword

DAVID ROBERT BAXTER
Superimposed Load Firearms
1360–1860 (South China
Morning Post, Hong Kong)

DOREEN BAXTER
Dreamland Frolics

DOW VAWTER BAXTER
Occurrence of Fungi in the
Major Forest Types of
Alaska
Some Resupinate Polypores
from the Region of the
Great Lakes
Importance of Fungi and
Defects in Handling Air-
plane Spruce

DUDLEY BAXTER
Cardinal Pole
The Holy Rood

E.B. BAXTER
The Essentials of Materia
Media and Therapeutics

EDNA DOROTHY BAXTER
An Approach to Guidance

EDWARD HENRY BAXTER
National Flags With Aircraft
Markings, Calendar of Days
for Hoisting National Flags
and Colour Keys for Ready
Identification

ELIZABETH BAXTER
The Healer
Sensitiveness and Its Cure

ERIC BAXTER
The Study Book of Coal

EVELYN VIDA BAXTER
A Vertebrate Fauna of Forth
Some Scottish Breeding Duck
The Birds of Scotland
Scottish Women's Rural
Institute Cookery Book

FRANK C. BAXTER
Days in the Painted Desert
and the San Francisco
Mountains

FRED BAXTER
Snake for Supper

GARRETT BAXTER
Baxter's Economics
Great Battles
Individualism
Powers

GEORGE BAXTER
Spiritualism—The Hidden

Peril, by an ex-medium (G.
Baxter)

GEORGE BAXTER
The Ballads of Mary Magda-
lene and Other Poems
The Pictorial Album; or
Cabinet of Paintings
Dawson's Book Shop, Los
Angeles

GEORGE OWEN BAXTER
Call of the Blood
Free Range Lanning
King Charlie
The Whispering Outlaw

GEORGE ROBERT
WYTHEN BAXTER
Humour and Pathos
The Book of the Bastiles, or
The History of the Working
of the New Poor Law
Don Juan Junior: A poem by
Byron's Ghost

SIR GEORGE
WASHINGTON BAXTER
Elk Hunting in Sweden

GILLIAN JOSE
CHARLOTTE BAXTER
The Perfect Horse
Horses in the Glen
Tan and Tarmac

GLAISTER BAXTER
The Agricultural Problems of
Panama

GLEN BAXTER
The Falls Tracer
The Khaki
Cranireons ov Botya
The Works
The Impending Gleam

Atlas

His Life: The Years of Struggle

Welcome to the Weird World of Baxter

The Billiard Table Murders

Glen Baxter Returns to Normal

The Collected Blurtings of Baxter

The Further Blurtings of Baxter

The Wonder Book of Sex

Blizzards of Tweed

Trundling Grunts

The Unhinged World of Glen Baxter

Loomings Over the Suet

Ominous Stains

GLEN WILLIAM BAXTER

Index to the Imperial Register of Tz'u Prosody, Ch'in-ting Tz'u-p'u

GORDON BAXTER

Vietnam: Search and Destroy

G.P. BAXTER

Researches Upon the Atomic Weights of Cadmium, Manganese, Bromine, Lead, Arsenic, Iodine, Silver, Chromium and Phosphorus

GREGORY PAUL BAXTER

Theodore William Richards

HAMILTON A. BAXTER

Blood Histamine Levels in Swine Following Total Body X-Radiation and a Flash Burn

Influence of Rapid Warming on Frostbite in Experimental Animals

HARRIET WARNER BAXTER

Poemscapes

HARRY BAXTER

Oboe Reed Technique

HAZEL BAXTER

Doctor in Doubt

Helicopter Nurse

HENRY FOSTER BAXTER

On Organic Polarity

HENRY WRIGHT BAXTER

A.C. Wear Tests on Low Voltage A.C. Contactor Tests

Calculated Curves of Inductive Energy at the Start of Arcing in Fuels

GEORGE YOUNG BAXTER JNR & HUBERT EUGENE BAXTER

Descriptive Geometry

HUGO F. BAXTER

Soi-disant. Poems with original drawings

IAN FRANCIS GEORGE BAXTER

The Law of Banking and the Canadian Bank Act

Essays on Private Law: Foreign Law and Foreign Judgements

IVY BAXTER

The Arts of an Island

J. BAXTER

A Toile for Two-legged Foxes

J. BAXTER

Statistics, Medical and Anthropological of the Provost-Marshal-General's Bureau derived from records of the examination for military service in the armies of the United States during the late War of the Rebellion of over a million recruits, drafted men, substitutes and enrolled men. Compiled under direction of the Secretary of War, Washington 1875

JAMES BAXTER

Culture of Harmony & Structure of Composition

Fires of No Return

JAMES ALBERT BAXTER

Accounting in a Building Stone Quarrying & Fabricating Business

JAMES CLEVELAND BAXTER

Mediated Generalization as a Function of Semantic Differential Performance

JAMES HOUSTON BAXTER

What to Read about Poland

Medieval Latin Word-List from British and Irish Sources—assisted by C. Johnson and Phyllis Abrahams

JAMES KEIR BAXTER

Aspects of Poetry in New Zealand

Autumn Testament

Recent Trends in New Zealand Poetry

Beyond the Palisade

The Iron Breadboard

Blow, Wind of Fruitfulness

The Bone Chanter

The Holy Life & Death of Concrete Grady

Pig Island Letters

Poems Unpleasant

The Rook Woman

JAMES PHINNEY BAXTER

The Elder George Cleeve of Casco Bay 1630–1667

The Present Status of Pre-Columbian Discovery of America by Norsemen

JAMES PHINNEY BAXTER

The Baxter Manuscripts

The Campaign Against the Pequakets

Three Suggestive Maps

Two Rhymes

Scientists Against Time

JAMES S. BAXTER

Development of the Female Genital Tract in the American Opossum

JAMES SIDLOW BAXTER

The Best Word Ever

JAMES SINCLAIR BAXTER

A Chapter on Irish Conveyancing

Aids to Embryology

JEAN LOGAN ROSE BAXTER

A 'Ae' Oo' etc (poems)

JEDEDIAH HYDE BAXTER

Statistics, Medical and Anthropological of the Provost-Marshall-General

JERE BAXTER

Reports of Cases argued and determined in the Supreme Court of Tennessee 1872 (9 vols)

JOHN BAXTER

An Appalling Talent: Ken Russell

The Cinema of John Ford

The Cinema of Joseph von Sternberg

The Gangster Film

King Vidor

Science Fiction in the Cinema

JOHN BAXTER

The Fire Came By; The Riddle of The Great Siberian Explosion

JOHN BAXTER

A Brief Description of Two Models of Improved Farmyard and Buildings with their advantages shown at the Industrial Exhibition in 1851

Baxter's Library of Agricultural and Horticultural Knowledge

JOHN BABINGTON MACAULAY BAXTER

Simon Baxter

Historical Records of the New Brunswick Regiment, Canadian Artillery

JOHN E. BAXTER

Locker Room Ballads

JOHN M. BAXTER

Marine Engine Pipe Arrangements

JOSIAH BAXTER

Mr. Baxter Baptiz'd in Bloud 1673

J.W. BAXTER

World Patent Law & Practice

KATHLEEN MARY CARVER BAXTER

Gerald of Wales (A play in 2 acts)

KATHERINE MARY BAXTER

Contemporary Theatre & The Christian Faith

KATHERINE SCHUYLER BAXTER

A Godchild of Washington, a Picture of the Past

KENNETH EUGENE BAXTER

Housing Standards in the U.S.A.

LAURA (FALKENRICH) BAXTER

Our Clothing

Today's Clothing

LUCY E. BAXTER

The Cathedral Builders

MRS LYDIA BAXTER

Gems By The Wayside (Poems)

MARTHA LEE BAXTER

The Uses of Motives in Beethoven Quartets

MARY BAXTER

The First Lady of the Tseng Clan

MARY DUDLEY BAXTER

The Story of a Robbery

MARY LISTER BAXTER

Songs of Sunset

MAURICE GLEN BAXTER

Daniel Webster & The Supreme Court

The Steamboat Monopoly

MICHAEL PAGET BAXTER
Forty Coming Wonders
Twelve Future Acts of Napoleon the Third

MILDRED FRAUNCES BAXTER
An Experimental Study of the Differential of Temperaments on a Basis of Rate and Strength

MURIEL BAXTER
The Voice of Truth

NATHANIEL BAXTER
Quaestiones et responsa in Petri Rami Dialecticam (with folding tables)

NEVINS D. BAXTER
The Commercial Paper Market

NICHOLAS HERBERT BAXTER
Natural Antiglobulin Antibodies in Primate Sera

NORMAN BAXTER
A Line on Texas

OLIVE BAXTER
Brave Little Nobody
Brooding Shadows
Capri Calling
The Jewel in the Cliff
Ken's Watery Shroud
Arrows of Jealousy
The Ashes of Sin
Debbie to the Rescue
The Raft of Death
Synthetic Halo

PATSY ANN LAYMAN BAXTER
The Explicit & Implicit Purposes of Samson Agonistes

PAUL TREVOR WILLIAM BAXTER
The Azande and Related People of the Anglo-Egyptian Sudan and Belgian Congo

PETER BAXTER
The Shoemaker
Incorporation of Perth

PHIL BAXTER
Moonlight and Shadows; A Book of Inspiratonal Rhymes (Amarillo)

RICHARD BAXTER
The Practical Works of the late Reverend and pious Mr. Richard Baxter
Richard Baxter's Account of his Present Thoughts con- cerning the controversies about the perseverance of the Saints. Occasioned by the gross misreports of some passages in his book, called The Right Method for peace of conscience and which are left out in the last impression to avoid offence
The Arrogancy of Reason against Divine Revelations repressed
Galwad ir Annychweledig idroi a byw

RICHARD BAXTER
The Body in the Kiosk
Stand By To Surface

ROBERT BAXTER
Doncaster Races
Irvingism — Its Rise, Progress & Present State
The Panic of 1866 With Its Lessons on The Currency Act

ROBERT DUDLEY BAXTER
The Re-Distribution of Seats in the Counties

RODERICK HILDEGAR BAXTER
The Quatuor Coronati Lodge, no. 2076

RONALD BAXTER
Giant in the Sun

SHANE V. BAXTER
Shadow of a Gunhawk

STEPHEN BARTOW BAXTER
The Development of the Treasury

S.T. BAXTER
Catalogue of Etruscan Jewellery with some Roman and Longobardic Ornaments

SYLVESTER BAXTER
La Arquitectura Hispano Colonial en Mexico
The Cruise of the Land Yacht
The Morse Collection of Japanese Pottery

THOMAS BAXTER (ATTORNEY GENERAL OF BARBADOS)
Letter from a Gentleman At Barbados (T. Baxter) to his friend now in London, concerning the administration of the Governor B-------g.

THOMAS PRESTON NOWELL BAXTER
Loneliness — An Address to the Members of the Girl's Friendly Society

THOMAS RICHARD BAXTER
Caribbean Bishops

T.S. BAXTER
Inghamite Chapel, Salterforth

T.W. BAXTER
Archival Facilities in Sub-Saharan Africa

VALERIE BAXTER
Young Policewoman

WALTER BAXTER
The Image and the Search (a novel)

WALTER RALEIGH BAXTER
The Calotype

WILLIAM BAXTER
Life of Knowles Shaw — The Singing Evangelist

WILLIAM BAXTER (CURATOR OF THE OXFORD BOTANIC GARDENS)
British Phoenogamous Botany

WILLIAM BAXTER
Commutator Construction
Hydraulic Elevators

WILLIAM BAXTER (MASTER OF THE MERCERS' SCHOOL LONDON)
Proposals for Printing by Subscription D. Guliemi Baxteri quae superstunt enarrationes & notae in D. Junii Juvenalis Satyras Accurante Mose Gulielmio

WILLIAM BAXTER (PRESIDENT OF ARKANSAS COLLEGE)
Pea Ridge and Prairie Grove

RT. HON. WILLIAM EDWARD BAXTER
Hints to Thinkers

WILLIAM EDWARD BAXTER
America and the Americans

WILLIAM EDWIN BAXTER
The Feathered Vocalist
Notes on the Practical Effect of Repealing the Newspaper Stamp Duty, the Advertising Duty and the Excise Duty on Paper

WILLIAM F. BAXTER
People or Penguins

W.G. BAXTER
Elijer Goff's Complete Works

WILLIAM HART BAXTER
Loudon's Hortus Britannicus

W.H. BAXTER
A True Friend to All Who Will Act the Part of a True Friend to One's Self

WILLIAM JOSEPH BAXTER
Chain Store Distribution and Management

WILLIAM JOSEPH BAXTER
Japan and America Must Work Together (1940)
No Inflation Coming (1946)

WILLIAM MORLEY BAXTER
The Sun and The Amateur Astronomer

WILLIAM RALEIGH BAXTER
The Handbook of Chemistry

WILLIAM SMITH BAXTER
Facts About Eyesight, Eyestrain and Spectacles

WILLIAM THOMAS BAXTER
Jewelry, Gem Cutting & Metalcraft

WILLIAM THRIEPLAND BAXTER
Depreciation
The House of Hancock

WINIFRED J. G. BAXTER
The Edinburgh Handbook of Housework

NEW AND FORTHCOMING TITLES
FROM NEW YORK REVIEW COMICS

AGONY
Mark Beyer

PEPLUM
Blutch

SOFT CITY
Pushwagner

PRETENDING IS LYING
Dominique Goblet

WHAT AM I DOING HERE?
Abner Dean

FOR SIX HAPPY YEARS I WORKED
AS POETRY EDITOR AT NYRB